Praise for *The Home Child*

'Liz Berry's *The Home Child* is an extraordinary work of imagination, conjuring the little-known stories of orphan children cast away from Britain to Canada. Poetic virtuosity is combined with novelistic storytelling as we follow the unfolding fate of Eliza Showell, an orphan girl from the 'Fiery Holes' of the Black Country, to the distant and hostile Marble Mountain. Berry's writing is beautifully in tune with childhood longing and fear, and the burning desire to love and belong. An exquisite book'

Hannah Lowe

'Only Liz Berry could write such raw and staggeringly beautiful poems, and bring such necessary, tender witness to the atrocities of child emigration. The reader is blown open to her home-child's world: cold skies, grief, a mother's love singing through the dark. This sequence broke my heart. Now little Eliza nests in its pieces'

Fiona Benson

'Every collection by Liz Berry is a treasure, but this one struck even deeper. The language is exquisite, every poem pitch perfect and brimming with tenderness; if there is rage in the heartbreaking story, the poetry breaks through it and transforms with love. And although the theme is personal, about a great aunt, this collection resonates with all who are exploited, abused, exiled and dispossessed. It has universal reach to the ongoing exploitation of Earth's poor. *The Home Child* is one of my favourite books of all time'

Pascale Petit

'I was gripped by *The Home Child* and endlessly delighted by Liz Berry's fierce and lovely reimagining of a forgotten life'

Alison Light

'These are beautiful poems that are full of compassion, inspired by a moment in our history that lacked compassion. Liz Berry has given the world another groundbreaking collection of poems. Her verses are sensitive and tender, yet the language is real and unflinching'

Benjamin Zephaniah

'The Home Child is a triumph. A novel in verse, an elegy, a profound act of witness, with the poet's enviable eye for image and detail. And like the best works of art and acts of witness it conveys dignity, a subtle and defiant humanity that rescues the forgotten, the wronged and the neglected from memory. It's a deep statement on the power and responsibility of writing, and I found it frequently moving, needfully shocking, and visionary and life-affirming in its metaphors. Eliza is brought to such tangible and complex life I feel as though I've met her'

Luke Kennard

'In The Home Child Liz Berry has produced a magnificent book that is a time machine, a memory-engine and a site for poetic narrative experiments. She takes us on a heartbreaking journey in a voice grown in Midland soil and thrown across the world, and she persuades us to examine our own past, whoever we are'

Ian McMillan

'Deeply moving. A graceful, delicate book, stunning in its emotional depth . . . I know I'll return to it many times in the future'

Megan Hunter

'These poems are as alive as fire, leaping from the page with vividness and warmth, their embers glimmering in the mind long after the book has ended. Deeply moving, unforgettable'

Doireann Ní Ghríofa

'The Home Child is a remarkable collection . . . This is poetry designed to rescue a girl from history – a thought-provoking weave of fact and imagination which tracks her as she adapts to this new world. It describes in her own words how her life is transformed and, in doing so, transforms ours'

John Glenday

'Liz Berry's poems are captivating and charged with her characteristically rich and sensuous Black Country language. The Home Child brings to light the devastating history of forced child migration in the service of Empire and is a deeply moving tribute to the author's great aunt. This is a book that should be on the curriculum'

Naush Sabah

THE HOME CHILD

THE HOME CHILD

A Novel in Verse

Liz Berry

Chatto & Windus
LONDON

1 3 5 7 9 10 8 6 4 2

Chatto & Windus, an imprint of Vintage, is part of the Penguin Random
House group of companies whose addresses can be found at
global.penguinrandomhouse.com

Penguin
Random House
UK

First published by Chatto & Windus in 2023

penguin.co.uk/vintage

A CIP catalogue record for this book is available from the British Library

HB ISBN 9781784742683

Typeset in 10/15 pt Quadraat OT by Jouve (UK), Milton Keynes
Printed and bound in Great Britain by Clays Ltd, Elcograf S.p.A.

The authorised representative in the EEA is Penguin Random House Ireland,
Morrison Chambers, 32 Nassau Street, Dublin D02 YH68

Penguin Random House is committed to a sustainable future
for our business, our readers and our planet. This book is made
from Forest Stewardship Council® certified paper.

For Eliza and all those who journey like her, with love

An Introduction

In 1908, aged twelve and newly orphaned, my great aunt, Eliza Showell, was sent from the Middlemore Children's Emigration Homes in Birmingham to rural Nova Scotia, Canada. She never returned to Britain or saw her brothers again.

This was not an uncommon story. Between 1860 and 1960, over 100,000 of Britain's poorest and most vulnerable children emigrated to Canada to work as indentured farm labourers and domestic servants. They were known as Home Children. Their migrations were arranged by religious missions, workhouse unions and philanthropic organisations. Some children were orphans, but most were from families who were unable to care for them due to poverty, illness or the loss of a working parent. It was believed that by sending the children to Canada they were being given the gift of a better life.

On arrival, Home Children were separated from any remaining family and received little supervision in their rural placements. Most worked only for their board and many were poorly treated. The children received scorn and abuse from the communities they entered, amid belief that, due to their circumstances, they were intellectually and morally unfit. Although some managed to thrive and build the promised 'better life' for themselves, many carried the effects of their loss and ill-treatment throughout their lives.

For Britain, the child migration schemes began as a philanthropic drive to save children from destitution. Yet emigration was also a cost-effective means of providing 'building blocks for the Empire', emptying overcrowded children's homes and ridding the country of those deemed to be a drain and threat to society. For Canada, Home Children provided a source of cheap labour. Indeed, the director of one agency involved in child migration argued that he did not believe the work of bringing British child migrants to Canada should be under the Department of Child Welfare but under the Department of Natural Resources.

The child migrant schemes were abandoned in the 1960s and evidence of them, and their failings, was buried until the late 1980s when the Child Migrants Trust began to uncover the stories of those sent away. Many of the children knew little of their birth families and had been made to feel so deeply ashamed of their pasts that they hid them even from their partners and families in adulthood. It is estimated that one in ten Canadians is now descended from a Home Child.

As for Eliza Showell, we know very little of her life beyond her Middlemore records, only that she lived all her years in the same small area of Cape Breton, working in domestic service, never raising a family of her own. We have two photographs of her: one as a young woman in the fields at Cape Breton, and one in old age, standing outside the white church at Marble Mountain. She died in a seniors' home in Inverness, Nova Scotia, in 1978. Her employers paid for a small stone to be laid for her in Malagawatch Cemetery. In 2010, the Canadian Year of the British Home Child, we visited the rural site where she is buried to lay wildflowers on her grave.

That same year, Prime Minister Gordon Brown made an official apology on behalf of the UK government to the child migrants and their families: 'We are sorry that they were allowed to be sent away at the time when they were most vulnerable. We are sorry that instead of caring for them, this country turned its back, and we are sorry that the voices of those children were not always heard.'

THE HOME CHILD

Children's Emigration Home
Birmingham, December 1907

A girl stands
  at the barred window
of 157 St Luke's Road,
  watching
snow fall upon
  the cobbled fode.

Her skin is freckled
  and pocked,
her shorn hair russet
  as a young fox.
Beneath her eyes –
  blue moons.

She is wearing
  a grey nightgown.
A bruise
  circles her wrist.
Snow enchants
  everything.

Is she singing?
  Praying? Calling
someone's name?
  Her eyelashes
upon the glass –
  dark wings in the frost.

Fiery Holes
Bilston, June 1907

Come by night, when spirits fly from the flames of the furnaces,
by night, barely darker than day, when the earth spews sulphur,
pounding and hammering, men stumbling
down its deepest seams,
a smutter of lamps, the drunken air.

Take the form of a moth, on shivering wings
take the wind, swift, to the court on Silver Street:
the passage, brew'us, stink of the miskin,
a windowpane cracked, laundry hung across each inch of the
        kitchen.
Here is the place. Damp walls, snuffed candle.

A child and her mother sweat beneath a blanket.
Thin as vixens. Both their hands raw from washing.
Eliza, the little stubborn one, is dreaming.
See the freckles twitch. See the dark of her lashes.
She dreams of horses:

the mare that draws the soil-cart through the reisty dark,
its silvery shoes agleam in the muck, the star on its brow.
She is in love with its prancing.
Curled against her mother's wheezing back
she digs her heels and dreams she is riding

bareback across the leasowe, beyond the town's rough hems,
her brothers, the steelworks, the sweltering chapel,
that terrible hovering rook of the workhouse.
Dreaming. Dreaming. The air blown spotless.
All the blackened sparrows lift their voices—

Eliza

Queen of all wet-the-beds and dander,
common nettles and dock,
sticklebacks, angle shades, sparrows, lice,
moles hung from nails like velvet gloves.
In the lezzer beyond the cut, see her –
queen of dung beetles and dog violets,
a crown on her head of all the town's daisies,
grime on their petal tips. Eliza
pursing her lips to a grass-blade,
calling up its music: come on come up!
The world is too alive to be down
in the dark, too afire, too fledgy.
Eliza's hair, dirty sorrel in sunlight,
lights the long grass ablaze.
Little queen of Fiery Holes,
with her back-to-back court, all its slum
and love, its cram like a burrow.
Eliza, queen of all lowly creeping souls,
all toilers and darklings. All shunned things
lay their blessings
at her wet and holey stockinged feet.
Long live the queen! Happiness is a wind
that whistles straight through.

Dandelions

We'm the wild little wet-the-beds
what grows in the cracks on the cut bridge,

a fistful of dazzle, ower high days spent blazing
atween blue brick and bibbles,

bright inspite everything, we bear
the world's rough boots, rise, sup rain,

crown the urchins, poor flowers,
who watch the osses drag the boats

down the cut. How calm they look,
blinkers fixing their eyes on the future.

But there's white at Mom's temples,
and the old elm's canting on the breeze –

blowball, clockflower, queen's crown, fortune teller
it's the winds now who'll carry us

hither and thither
and all across the Seven Cornfields like seeds.

September

The osses know it.

The sparrows know it.

Me, on my back beneath the wych elm, knows it.

There are some who'll be lent to us
only in dream.

Cru cruel cru, the pigeon's warning.

What'll we do, Jim? Tell me. What'll we do?

Black Ribbon

Babby little babby, Mom kisses me goodnight,
    soap and Dolly Blue, suds swilling the fode all silver,

brushes my hair, pulls me close
    as the sun on the violets. *Eliza. 'li-za.*

Out in the dark – the factories ommering,
    the soil-oss prances er fancy clop,

but inside it's just us, singing the chapel songs:
    God Sees the Little Sparrow Fall,

and er doesn't cry, just holds my ond
    til the floor is air and like birds we'm flown – –

then light at the pane, someone bowing
    my head to whisper 'poor wench'

and tie a borrowed black ribbon
    round my skull.

Children's Emigration Homes Case Report
Eliza Showell, November 1907

Mother dead, father long deceased. Girl 12 was living
with her two brothers
aged respectively 16 (James/Jim) 14 (Samuel) years
in the house & all occupied one bedroom &
slept in the same bed. Conditions unsanitary.
Girl no longer attending school.
The case was brought under the notice
of Inspector S. Moran NSPCC who threatens
to prosecute the elder brother unless
he allows the girl to be removed.

Description: Nice bright-looking girl, rather short.
To be taken in.

Admission

All night sparrows flitting through my lungs. I close my face like the petals of a daisy. Mom O Mom O Mom O— All them little wenches wi their nosy-bugger eyes, gawping as the matron lifts her silver scissors. Piss off, I spits, my donny clamped to my lips, too late . . .

A word is not a sparrow; once it flies out it cannot be caught.

★

She bows her head
and the eyes of the birds gaze
upon it,

a field of stubble
after harvest,
the chaff blown.

Only wind to kiss it now,
shivering her scalp
so pale beneath.

In the dormitory at night

a garden of girls is blooming,
the hum of their hearts like bees

in swarm, thrumming thrumming,
their dreams overgrown and blown to seed,

sorrow's blackbird high in the wych elm
sings. Lily. Camelia. Ivy. Rose.

Poor flowers of the field:
wrong soil, worst season,

that winter chiller than ever was known,
the slums bone-dead.

Here's Iris, scrawny as a seedling,
skin gold in the creeping dawnlight.

Daisy, the drunk's girl, bruised, thin,
hair shorn to a fuzzed halo.

Olive, with her made-up blasphemous prayer
that cools the air like rain.

How their tendrils unfurl from their narrow beds,
reach out through the darkness.

Bloom where you are planted,
the sampler tells them. But o their voices –

flowers torn from their black roots
and laid on a grave.

Children's Emigration Homes Case Report
Eliza Showell, January 1908

Summary: Girl already used to some schooling
and domestic work (mother – deceased – a washerwoman).
Manners rough but likely improved on arrival.

Proceed: To Canada

Travelling Case

Eliza Showell

-Middlemore-

3 nightgowns, 3 chemises, 3 pairs drawers, 2 white petticoats, 2 flannel petticoats, 3 pairs unbleached cotton stockings, 3 cotton frocks with long sleeves and pockets, 2 linsey frocks, 1 warm petticoat for voyage, 1 plain brown ulster, 3 pinafores, 1 straw hat for Sundays, 1 blue hood for voyage, 2 pairs boots, 1 brush and comb, 3 pocket handkerchiefs, 1 bag, 1 Bible, 1 Common Prayer Book, 1 case 2ft by 1 1/2 ft to hold everything.

Sailing Day, Liverpool

The gulls am crying like little wenches.

goodbyegoodbyegoodluckgoodbye

Raw and squaily, the wind mithers
as we climb the steps,
birdy legs ashiver
in our itchy new stockings.

Nellie, Margaret, Kathleen, Dora.   *Age 4, 9, 6, 11.*
Higgins, Showell, Elwell, Proctor.

White hankies whipped
from our waving onds,
   quick as birds
      flying up up.

     'We'm off!'

Only Dora Pike blarting,

Agnes, Eliza, Peg, Hilda.   *Age 3, 5, 12, 7.*
Bibb, Gell, Hodgetts, Mundon.

the rest of us ghosty-faced,
so quiet
you can hear our bellies jimmuck
as the waves rock the ship,

goodbyegoodbyegoodluckgoodbye

watching Liverpool shrink
to a doll's town in the fog,
already wiping out
the sight of us,

Doris, Rose, Ida, Clara
Dakin, Tomkins, Pike, Bunder.

us herded like cows
down   endless   wet   steps,
squeezing the ond
of the wench in front.

goodbyegoodbyegoodriddancegoodbye

Dear Sir,

I am asking after my sister, Eliza Showell. I know she was
to be taken to your home in Birmingham for schooling until
I am able to aford better sircumstanses.

Yours gratefuly,

James (Jim) Showell

Voyage

Eleven days, eleven nights
nothing but the waves
and my shivering guts and
Dora Pike blarting
and the – and the –
and the way I bite my tongue til it bleeds
and and—
shut that memory like a midden door.

S/S *Carthaginian*, Allan Line

Mrs Cready, the chaperone, gives us a postcard
of a ship: S/S *Empress of Canada*.
Not even our ship.
So saft they think us, that we'll believe any lie.
I don't know why but I keep it,
slide it in the back of my Common Prayer
and stare at it each night
when I kneel on the splintery boards
to say *Ower Father*,
and look at it every night after til I feel so old.

Ower Father, who art not in this ship,
who art not in the sweat and whining of this hold,

don't forget us, your wenches,
don't let us die of the sickness,

don't let us drown like dogs in the cut.

My last babby tooth

comes out on a string of skin,
yellow and brown as a wet-the-bed,
a butterfly of blood.
After breakfast, me and Dora
throw it overdeck, all the waves singing
their churny song.
O Dora, don't you wish
we could jump in after it, down
into the foam
to be swallowed by a clam,
then held and shined
til we was spotless
and precious as pearls.

Dear Jim

Your sister Eliza

Dear _Mr Showell_ ,

I am desired to inform you that in accordance with the terms of Agreement entered into when _Eliza Showell_ was received into our institutions, the managers have included her in a party of girls who left these Homes for Canada ~~yesterday~~ _last month_. We have been unable to reach you at the address previously provided.

Should you desire to write to the child her address is c/o

_____

I am directed to inform you that in Canada she will be under the same kind and watchful supervision as she would have enjoyed had she remained in England.

The Managers have every reason to believe that her best interests will be served by her emigration.

Yours faithfully,

Mr C Barker

Immigration Shed
Halifax, Nova Scotia

Place of birth?

Silver Street, Bilston, I says.
I've got two brothers, I says. Jim'll write for me, I says.
I wo' be stopping here, I says.

He measures me, looks at my teeth,
pushes a cold metal listener to my chest
and barks: *cough.*

I wo' be stopping here, I says.
I've got two brothers. Write it. Silver Street, Bilston.
He lifts my eyelids.

Calls:
Infirmary.

Infirmary

She went down to the Infirmary, a snowdrop in a row,
planted deep in the Infirmary, an iron-bedded row,
so cold, so sweet, so fair, a girl, a snowdrop in the snow.

Let her go, let her go.

That night in the Infirmary a fever it did moan,
in her little cotton nightgown, the fever it did moan,
so cold, so sick, so pale, that girl, like snow dropped in her
     bones.

Let her go, let her go.

The dove that slept within her chest was taken by a crow,
that dove, so meek, within her breast, it changed into a crow,
so cold, so strange, so wild, this girl, a shadow on the snow.

Let her go, let her go.

At dawn in the Infirmary, a wind began to blow,
round the walls of the Infirmary, a chill wind it did blow:
so cold, so young, so poor, our girl, won't someone let her go?

Let her go, let her go.

God bless her, let her go.

Sparrows

I wake up drenched wi sweat, teeth rattling, the dream still
running silver through me, silver ribbon of the cut, tumble-
down court on Silver Street, snow slushing to silver in the
fode, close as sweethearts – me and Mom – the way er onds
flutter up in the air like little sparrows as er turns to me and
says *gi us yo donny, mah wench* and I hold out my palm for er
kiss, er warmth making a candle of me, everything softening,
then just as we'm touching—

Fairview, Receiving Home
Halifax

The alders rattle their bony fingers at the windows.

I cover myself wi my onds and keep my eyes on them trees

as we'm scrubbed one by one in a metal tub.

A clean white pinna laid across the chair, a metal bed,

the smell of piddle and violets.

All of us kneeling. Our Mothers who art in heaven.

Saying your prayers ay the same as praying.

Her Name

I lock it up in my heart
((Adelina))

Shivering mountain flower.

Lifted from the filth
and toil of Fiery Holes,
to a cove of pearl.

Our Lady of the Weeping.

Mom, Mom—

The Word

a girl is coming to McPhail's farm
   a girl a girl is coming to the farm a Home girl
      a girl is coming to the farm yes to the farm
   to McPhail's a girl to do the housework
the hefting work a girl now Suki is abed
   but a girl one of those girls *those* girls
up at McPhail's yes filthystreetrats all
a girl coming guttersnipes coming coming to the farm
   Ali must want his head read
 the ice not yet Suki still abed coming to the farm
a girl is coming a girl coming a girl but who?

A Girl

A girl is a new penny in the satin slit of a purse.

A girl is a bulb, greedy for light, in the clem-gutted earth.

A girl is a crowning-in, the soil's O, the panicked shaft.

A girl is a glede, ready to ignite, in the restless ash.

A girl is a pit oss, a thrush, a white ferret, a lark.

A girl is cream rising thick as desire in the dark.

Girl Number 383, Alastair McPhail's farm,
nr Marble Mountain

Sound in wind and limb.
A little thin I admit

but her teeth are strong
and her mane clean of lice.

The wiry ones grow tough
when worked, earn their keep,

bow their heads, learn to close
their jaws upon the bit.

Marble Mountain

Twin churches perched on the roadside
like two white doves, eyes shut
and beaks to the sun.

Where were you brought from, lassie?
I says: wum.

McPhail's

The cart rattles us
as it rides the rough cobbles,
out from the town
to the dirt road
wicked wi bibbles.
White dust spockling everywhere.
My voice shut-up
like a jack-in-the-box
waiting to pop out.
What do they call you? he says.
Eliza, I says.
Lizzie then, he says.
This here's the farm.

I keep my eyes on the floor,
its birls of white dust,
as Mr McPhail smooths
his white moustache
in a small cracked looking glass
on the shelf.
He don't believe in vanity,
thieving, lying, gossiping,
lazing, cussing
(or any crimes
belonging to wenches).

Mind that, he says,
or we'll send you back
so quick
your boots'll burn.

His wife Suki is in bed,
weak as a lamb,
I must wash er silver hair
wi pine water
and wind its ghosty wool
into a bun.
Coddle er like a babby.
Er blue eyes am rheumy
as a kitten's.
Er chest wheezes
wi the churchyard cough.

What do they call you? er says,
beckoning me to the bed.
I lift my eyes to ers.
Eliza, I whisper.
Lizzie, er creaks.
Come here to me, Lizzie.
I move closer.
The smell of violets
and summat sharp
clagging my throat.
Er catches olt of my ond.

Lizzie, er says, you
and this place
better shine like pins.

I Serve in Duty for the Blessing of Our Lord

Rise afore cockcrow. Light the fire, fill the pails from the creaking pump. Slop the pig and the piglets. Turn out the hens, feed and water them, put my ond under the reisty straw for their eggs. Warm Mrs McPhail's milk in a babby's tin cup. Sweep the floors of lime dust. Strain the milk. Cook the breakfast – pancakes, eggs, sweet tea. Wash the dishes. Tend to Mrs McPhail. School (if needed) a mile and a half down the muddy track. Black the grate. Make bread (cackonded). Sweep the floors. Turn the beds. Hoe the weeds. Cook supper and serve it. Wash the dishes. Slop the pigs. Fasten up the hens. Dish up oats for the foal. Tend to Mrs McPhail. Wash myself, say my prayers. Our pigging father. Dream of running away. Dream of thieving the mare and running running to god knows where. Mom, O Mom. Then wum, black as the lake, far gone, in the thick lampless dark.

Out West

The land swallowed them,
guttled them, spat out their dreams,
broke their bones with its wintery teeth, its frozen farms,
gobbled them into the loam like bad seeds
and let the worms comfort them;
there, inspite the drought and the flood,
the hostile roots of the spruce,
the teeth of voles in the autumn mulch,
their green shoots pushed up
into the wild blue, to the love of the sun.
Walk across the hills of Whycocomagh
when the light near blinds you
and you will see them in the furrows,
in the heartsore violets, the shivering pines.

Nellie Higgins

Rose Elwell

Dora Pike

Margaret Proctor

Agnes Bibb

Ivy Gell

Peg Hodgetts

Hilda Mundon

Dolly Shaw

Olive Dakin

Clara Tomkins

Lily Bunder

Wandering

In the quiet afore tea I go wandering,
tramping the fields,
catch the blossom coming off the branches like snow.

I ay never knowed a place like this afore.
Breeze that boxes your ears wi bee hum,
hush-hush grasses, them little jewel birds in the air.

I spy on the quarry, lime dust blowing up
in great white clouds, men turned ghosts,
the boats crossing the lake like needles through cloth.

I'm waiting for Jim's letter. Like he promised.
When he let em take me away.
My hair still long. The earth still churned on Mom's grave.

Snowed

In the lezzer beyond the farms,
the slopes am wild wi flowers,
ox eye, sow's snout,
all snowed white with marble dust,
white as the winter fode,
and when I step atween em
my boots am snowed,
my shins am snowed,
the raw scrapes on my knees
am snowed;
and I lie down in em,
my pinna hitched up to my drawers,
and the dark places, the red places,
the places where I burn and burn,
they all am snowed.

The Creatures

When there's no light left
and my bones am sore

I visit the babby foal,
bright and black as a seam of coal,

stroke er neck til er gleams.
I ay got no one, I tells er.

No one who's mine now.
Only you.

Thaw

If Mrs McPhail's lungs wheeze
I must help er raise er shoulders

beckon out the cough.

Er chest rattles, er hair looses
from its bun.

Er grips my ond
and looks at my eyes so sorry

it makes me afeared.
We can hear it. The church bell.

Er spits in the basin,
turns to the wall wi er wet blue eyes

and wipes er lips on the sheets
I have scrubbed in the sun.

Silence settles between us like snow.

I had a child once, Lizzie –
she didn't live past the frost.

Mom

On Marble Mountain er lies with me
in the shivery dark, whiter than lime
in er one good nightgown.
Er smooths my hair a hundred strokes
wi a hardbacked brush.
Some nights er waits for me in frost,
er onds scratching at the barn like birds.
Er sings to me, in the milkweed and goose grass,
in the horse cack and bucket's slop,
when I kneel and work.
Er is always singing
Tis So Sweet To Trust,
and though my onds am raw
and my mouth is a donkey's,
good for nothing but straw,
I say er name, er beautiful name, er name
like a song, *Mom, Mom,*
til it turns to *wum.*

Moon

And here is the moon.

A pail of cream left out in the frost.

Do you remember it, Suki?

A child's name written in milk
upon water.

This, they say, is the loneliest colour.

B is for Book

What's your real name, girl? says Mrs McPhail
in er ghosty voice.
Eliza, I says.
In the yellow light
the sun flitting through the branches,
through the curtains,
like little birds, er looks at me
as I turn er blankets.
You book-learned, Lizzie?
Yes, I says, a bit.
Then bring the reader from the shelf.

I sit beside er bed
on a low wood milking stool,
the tatty *Girls' Reading Book*
trembling in my onds
B is for book, which to – guide us is given. –
Though written – by men the – words came from heaven.
Suki reaches er ond
towards my ond.
Er skin feels like paper.
That'll do, er says.
The tears spill quiet down er face
like thaw.

Tis So Sweet To Trust

Ower Father
who art in wum
bless the tunky pig
and piglets fat as butter
bless their slop and muck
bless the cows   the white one most
and er coddly milk   bless the barn the hay
bless the ribbony black foal
give er opples and straw
give er the run of the road
bless the lake's wet gold
and the boats full of marble
bless the two white churches
the scrawny birling cockerel
bless me   Eliza Showell
make me grateful and glad
bless my brothers
bless my mom
in the windy bone-orchard
bless Bilston   bless ower fode
bless the soot on ower fode
mek me sweet and dark as the soot
on ower poor fode
mek me hardworking Lord
mek me fit for heaven

whiter than the quarry
mek me good for Mrs McPhail
mek me good for my own sake
mek me pure God   mek me good
for at dusk in the barn
when the moon's the only lantern
and the mice am singing
I roll in the straw like a babby piglet
and everything in me squeals
to be bad

They say

A Home girl in Baddeck put arsenic in the well
    and the farmer drank from it.

A Home boy in Whycocomagh threatened
    his master with a stolen shotgun.

A Home boy in Grand River set ablaze to the barn
    and burnt its bones to black dust.

A Home girl in Strathlorne bore her shame
    into the snow and the farm-wife buried it.

Darling Foal

She was lonely, little foal,
and the loneliness was so deep,
a field chest-high of snow
she stumbled through, shivering;
a night without stars or moon.
It was so deep, little foal,
that she would never know the bottom.
It was so deep inside her.

When she stroked you
and kissed you, her bony fingers
lifting the rough hairs
of your mane, she was lost
in that meadow, snow-blind, fumbling,
but holding your skittery body
to her chest, she held
her foal heart, its dark blessing
a-burn inspite the blizzard.

Mr James Showell
3 Silver Street, Bilston

c/o Middlemore

Dear Jim,

I hope you am quite well
as I am myself. I am writing
from Canada. They have sent me
to Canada. My place now
is Marble Mountain,
a quarry with boats coming
and going and men
from about every place.
My people am farmers
and decent ~~enough~~
~~but work me so hard~~
~~my bones crack at night.~~
The woman is kinder.
I am to go to school.
Will you send ~~for me?~~
me news from home
for I am – quite well
and happy and ever so

58

~~lonely~~ grateful, yes ever so –
quite well and happy.
Lord bless us all.
Jim, ~~will~~ should you look for me –
they call me by a different name.
They call me Lizzie McPhail.
I must tell you that I am quite
well and happy.

Your loving sister,
Eliza x

The Naming of the Saints

Oh white wooden clapboard church amongst the pine trees.

Oh church atween the long grasses. Place of rushing rain,

its hush hush song. A dream she cannot wake from.

In the pew at the back, she cradles her fists to look like prayer.

But she never prays here, only names her saints: the foal,
    the goose,

the hummingbird that hovers at the hem of the summer,
    and always Adelina

plaiting the burning rope of her hair with hands of cool water.

Forerunners / Premonition

Here it comes again: the wheezing lungs
of the organ, the voices low and canting.
God sees the little sparrow fall.
Eliza sits upright in bed, sweating.
No light in the yard,
no light on the path but the snuffed stars.
There are things that appear only
beyond the burning of dusk,
poked from the embers of night.
The undertaker paid in rabbits
and wrung-necked cockerels.
The cart dragged by mares,
rime pearling their nostrils.
Eliza hears her own heart drumming
as the room peels back like fog
from the lake. The wall clock stopped,
the looking glass veiled in thick soot.
Then her nose punched by violets,
her words unlinking
scattering like teeth into the dark pines
for the dogs to find.
Who is carrying that coffin?
Who is lying inside?   Who is going – again –
to a grave with no name?

They say

A farmer in Inverness
    flogged his Home boy with a horse whip
for speaking ill of the food.

A woman in Louisbourg
    pressed her Home girl's hand to the griddle
for spilling milk from the pail.

A prison guard in Antigonish
    locked his Home child in the attic for eight days
with only bread and water.

A farmer in Sydney
    sent his Home girl packing with a greater burden
than the one she'd arrived with.

Snow Globe

Imagine her in the snow globe of the first winter when the snow falls for months, when the wind is a coyote at the barn doors and the Scotch pines are furred like great bears. The water in the trough is ice, the little speckle-bellied fish motionless in the stream and the only sounds in the muffled woods are of snow falling (but that is no sound at all) and Eliza's breath on the wet wool of her collar (and that too is no sound at all). The whiteness changes everything, everything is wiped away: the backroads, the churches, the dead returning to loam in the Malagawatch Cemetery, even the lake itself has been drunk by whiteness. Only she has colour – that sorrel hair like a bird from the old country.

Shake the glass globe and watch her in miniature: cradling a piglet, mucking out in the syrupy light of the late sun, or curled on her side on her narrow cot, eyes open, mouth ajar, watching her breath freeze in the air.

No matter how we shake, the snow will still fall, the foal suck milk from her fingers in the stable, the violets lift their trembling shoots from the earth. The snow falls. It is happening still. The snow falls as if it will never stop falling. Somewhere, somewhere we choose not to look.

Look she is crying. Now shake again and her tears melt like snowflakes on her cheeks.

Suki

Lizzie, when I was young, we'd dance
    in McAuliffe's barn, the animals cleared out
and lanterns hung. How it smelled of cattle
    and the lavender balm
we rubbed our throats with then,

a good deal of moonshine;
    Charlie McAuliffe playing fiddle
and the Stewarts' boy – long buried now – working
    the accordion like he was waltzing
with a lassie. Jigs, reels, stripping

the willow. The night burning harder.
    The barn like a glow-worm in the country-dusk
seeking its darling. I was the sweetheart
    of Matthew McColl then.
How dark his hair was, like a pebble

under water, oh when we danced,
    my skirts swung and my hair loosed
its ribbons in a way most improper.
    Oh Lizzie, those nights –
we walked home between the maples,

the thaw dripping,
    all the branches tangling like new-weds—

Trembling Aspen

You might see her, at gloaming,
when the sun stains the furrows rose-gold
and the barn swallows are careening;
you might catch her between the trees
behind McPhail's old place,
beyond the barn – now in ruins –
where she worked that filthy spring.

She is shivering, shot by light, haloed
by midges, move closer
until you are sure she is no longer a girl
but a trembling aspen,
taller than you'd dreamt her,
slender back like woodsmoke
in her grey work pinafore.

See how she quivers at the whip
of a twig, the loose-change *chuch*
of a redpoll in her boughs.
See how singular she is
amongst her sisters in the forest
though their moans are the same papery hum:
a library being read by a thousand young women.

In the Schoolroom

If Margaret has three apples and the horse takes one,
how velvet will its lips be
as it presses them to the pips?

If Susan bakes five pies and takes three to her mother
in Malagawatch Cemetery,
how lonely will the house of the spirits be?

★

My script on the workbook
like a scraggy goose foot
crossing the snowed field.
Nothing like a lady's.

The ink smudged, goose
stumbling and slipping,
snow angel
in its warm pool of thaw.

★

Three times snow is snow
      dirty bitch
Four times rain is rain
      streetrat
Five times her heart ashiver
      guttersnipe
Six times it thaws again.

Teacher's Report:
The girl has little to say and when she does speak
her voice is rather guttural and difficult to understand,
quite the sound of a navvy grinding lime in the quarry.

The Owd Words

Sweet wum gob.
Like pearls my mouth gleams
wi the owd words,
my tongue strung –
fittle jeth ketch
words like a kiss, a pit,
a fruit-stone in my throat,
words filthy as the soot,
steaming as the *miskin*,
words that wake me
wailing in the dawn,
thrape, opple, mom,
babby. That metal taste
of blood, a bad penny.

The Storm / Charm for a Lonely Girl

Pick a sprig of yarrow, put the stem up your nose, and say:

Yarrow yarrow, if he loves me and I loves he,
a drop of blood I'd wish to see.

If blood appears, it shows you are loved.

⋆

Let us kneel, let us pray, let the storm rattle the shingles,
shake the windows from their frames.
The first curse stain on her pinafore, a shot dove in a field of
　　　snow.

⋆

Suki tells me to cut some rags from the old bedsheet.
Soak them in cold salt water after.
It's your monthly, er says, your curses.
Did nobody ever tell you?

⋆

Say, in the woods after dark, holding the tip of a leaf –
Low for a foreigner,
Bark for a near one,
Crow for a farmer,
Screak, tree, screak, if I'm to die first.

The Word

a boy is coming to McPhail's farm
    a boy   a boy is coming to the farm a boy
      a boy is coming to the farm yes to the farm
    a boy no a boy this time to McPhail's
     a boy   the ice not yet thawed on the trough
but a boy   from Glasgow a streetrat   yes McPhail's farm
   one of those boys   *those* boys up at McPhail's yes
coming a boy coming to the farm some folk never learn
   the ice not yet coming to the farm a boy guttersnipe
is coming a boy coming a boy a boy but who?

First Sight

He keeps his eyes on the floor,
onds behind his back.

> (I can hear his breathing)

Do what you're told, lad,
keep your hands to yourself.

> (He stutters, his words
>   a cart stuck on a cobble)

No thieving, lying, cursing, spitting,
brawling, insubordination.

> (His hair is the colour
>   of wheat at harvest)

One slip and you're out,
back where you came from.

> (I read the label on his coat:
>   Boy 131: Daniel McFadden)

I know your kind, do y'hear?
Y-yes sssir, I do sir.

> (His voice. I tasted it –
>   syrup in my throat)

Keyhole

In the poky attic, he has arranged his tranklements
like a little chapel.

I spy on it when I sweep the house
of lime dust and spiders.

One thin brown coat, one peaked cap,
a Bible hidden in his trunk (pages torn)

and a photograph of a woman,
smiling shy, cracked at the corners.

Does he dream of er when he sleeps?
Er soft frock, the wave of er hair.

I imagine his head laid on that thin grey pillow –
honey on the comb.

The First Pear

All day we'm kept separate. Me in the kitchen, him in the
      yard.
Me in the yard, him in the barn. Me in the barn, him in the
      field.

I eat at the table. Him, on a wooden crate by the range.
In church we kneel, the McPhails atween us.

But sometimes, when he thinks they don't see, he hovers
on the stair to listen when I'm reading,

trails me as I walk the lonely path to school. Sometimes, I
leave his breakfast on the step. Once – the first pear.

Daniel

A boy is a photograph of his mother,
her face rubbed to gold,

a handmade shiv
in the trunk's secret fold,

a name knifed
into the maple's dripping bark,

a stream, chill and slaking,
cussing through the dark.

A boy is a rattle-boned wammel,
a whelpling, a loon,

the shudder of the lake
as it's entered by moon,

a prayer for a thunderstorm
in August's long heat,

that first pear, on his tongue,
ungodly sweet.

In the Pines

Meet me in the pines, he says,
  and so I go
in the pink sky of dawn, wench's sky,
  the night lifting
      like a mourning veil,
  the dew trembling on the ferns
so quiet, no one knowing
  even the animals still snuffling in their straw.
My boots am sodden,
  my heart ommering in my chest,
  I can smell the pines all sweet,
  the quarry –
and he's there, smiling,
  teeth like babby teeth, his eyes lit-up.
You came, he says.
  I nod. Pines shushing me quiet.
Feel this, he says,
  touching a leaf to my fingers,
  they call it a lamb's ear.
And it's soft, so soft,
that when I fold it in my palm,
  the tears come like rain.

★

The rain that falls on Lammas Day
shall cure
even the sorest eyes
made raw by weeping.

★

Evening chores done.
Sitting on the back step, the rain so soft
you hardly know you're soaked.
Lizzie isn't my real name.   *Oh?*
That's what they call me here
but my real name was Eliza.   *Oh.*
And he says it, says it, says it so soft
it's mizzle kissing my eyelids.

Canting

When we can, we talk. Canting canting canting
until it feel so sweet. His Mammy. My Mom.

(My mouth full of opples.)

About my brothers. Wum. Fiery Holes.
The ship in all that wind and sickness.

How I read to Suki. How I'm frightened of er dying.
How I run my finger across the cream when no one's looking.

(His mouth full of opples.)

His sister in Maryhill, who'll come for him,
he says, when er's earned the money.

He writes to er each night though he never posts them.
He's been placed before, in Antigonish,

where the farmer beat him, made him sleep in the hay
til his lips turned blue.

He spat in the milk and ran away. Was made to beg
for McPhail to take him, turn him decent.

(Our mouths sweet with opples.)

Cant cant cant. Like the crows in the fir trees,
the lake slapping the harbour. The osses whinnying

and careening round the pasture
when the wind whips them to wild dreaming.

Foal

For one hundred and forty-seven days
no one touched her,
no one brushed her hair,
no one rocked her or soothed her,
no one rubbed balsam into her back
when the cough rattled her lungs,
no one caught her arm to halt her
as she skittered from the barns,
no one took her hand,
traced their name and a heart
on the sapling of her spine,
no one until he came
through the meadowy dusk
where she crouched in the stable,
lifting a bridle, her sorrel head
bowed, her teeth clacking
as he knelt before her
and touched his fingers to her mane.

The Gift

A scarlet ribbon,
coiled tight in his palm
pressed into mine.

He took it
from the counter
of Stewart's Store.

Nobody ever gave me
anything
so beautiful.

Underneath my pillow
it glows all night.
Little fire.

Oh Sweethearts

And slowly we'm sweethearts
atween the wet grass all river-licked,
lime dust in our hair
and both of us so frightened,
blind as moles. But wanting
something. Wanting.
We'm side-by-side on the grass,
my barefeet in the water
bowing our heads, gentle
as osses at the water-trough.
I can feel his shoulder ashiver
and it makes me bold, makes me jumpy,
so I hold out my ond
til he takes it and kisses the palm
like he's eating sugar from it
and we'm off . . .

Barefoot

In the long days I go barefoot,
across the parched grass,
across the yard, its wicked bibbles,
where the little black filly kneels in the sun,
over the moss, the gushy stream,
the loam and the wench-faced violets.
They'd hardly know me now
wi my brown feet tough as hooves,
my ankles all fur and skinny as the oss's
when once upon a moon in Bilston
they was white and soft as ghost fish.
But oh, it grows so cold in the night
that my poor toes am frozen,
pinned and needled til I sob
thinking how they poked from the bed
where we all snored like piglets,
how Mom'd rub the life into them.
Oh, Mom, that er would come now
and see he loves me like er did
for, come dawn, he pokes the sweetest heifer
from er bed – hefting er dozy bulk
and chobbling dream grass –
then makes a nest from the straw
and buries my feet inside til they hatch
to life like babby snow geese.

There is a Land of Pure Delight

The good and fancy of the town
am up at Whalers Point
picnicking and praying,
chobbling lobster sandwiches,
their Sunday School clothes
grand in the sun.

What do they know
of heaven, when we'm in heaven
down here? A nest of warm grass,
the stream's long drink
and blueberries, sharp and guttly,
giddying our lips
like we'm canting of love.

In the Stable

Eliza, little horse bride,
mane starred with meadowsweet,
the wedding-wind gusting violets
and the ripe, butterflying perfume
of horse muck. Eliza,
kneeling as if she is vowing,
her wedding shoes dainty
silver crescents, her ring a bridle.
She nibbles carrots and soft red apples
for her bride feast, puts her cheek
to a forelock and oh –
the suede of his lips on her palm,
hay-breath warm behind teeth
crooked as the gravestones
in Malagawatch bone-orchard.
Mother, father, brother, husband.
What tenderness is this, what lonely love?
Shut the stable doors and let them lie
until cockcrow, safe and chaste
in their bridebed of straw and wild grasses,
the parish-lantern keeping watch
like a fretful new mother, the mice singing
their songs of sowing and harvest.

White Ribbon

He has a scar across his shoulders
from being caned
in the receiving home
for refusing to pray.
I touch my fingertip to it:
a white ribbon.
Oh Brightest and Best
of the Sons of the Morning

Suki grips my wrist as I'm washing er.

Don't mess around with boys, Lizzie.
Nothing good will come of it.

Red Ribbon

Holding his hand in the barn,
the hot breath of the calves between us,

it unspools from my heart
to tie our bodies in the dark.

Lizzie, he says, *one day we'll get married,*
have our own home.

Lake shimmering gold in the sun.
Lake shivering silver in the moon.

And what shall you call it?

Who Art in Heaven

I wake in the velvety thickness of cockcrow,
sweat soaking my ribs.
He's stirring, creaking boards, his cough.
Someone is shouting.
Daniel. Daniel. My skin burns.
I slip my fingers inside my pocket
to feel for the ribbon's cool silk—

—but it's gone–the ribbon–it's gone–it's gone–who has
　　it–where is it–the ribbon is gone—

Come on, he says

and we'm running
        running
through the high grass and the fireweed
  beyond the barns   the lezzer
       swift
over the stream   the fence
   my hair in my eyes
     spit flecking at my lips

they'll send us back, he says
  Lizzie, they will

so we'm running
  through the pines, the glade
    the crows crying
       go on go on

my fingers burning in his grip
  so tight
    he's pulling me
    come on come on
    they've seen us
   his chest wheezing
    my heels slamming the red dirt

then we'm tumbling
  pain like a trap
   my ankles twisting

but he doesn't let go
  crouches beside me
   breath rasping

come on Lizzie, he says,
   and he's looking
    at my face
   but I'm blarting now
  and the dawn's coming

and we know it –
   it's done.

Moonlight

He sleeps that night in the barn.
No candle or lantern for McPhail is afeared he'll set fire to it.

The animals shift in the moony dark,
sigh out their steam and grassy breath.

I press my face to the glass, nothing but the darkness
and the stars who never say anything.

What's to be said? Tears sodden my nightgown.
Will they send me on too? To what?

To who? A girl of thirteen rolls around
like a bad penny no one wants to save.

Suki calls me to her bedside. *You'll stay Lizzie*, er wheezes,
er eyes am wet and er mouth trembly.
I need you.
But the boy must go.

The sunbeams flit into my eyes, across my face until I'm
        blinded,
moving like moths
into the locked drawers of my heart.

Wolfville

They sent him away on the dawn train to Wolfville,
her blackbird, her boy, on the dawn train to Wolfville,
now no wind can ever blow here but ill.

The train was black and its heart was a firebox,
black as the Bible, its heart was a firebox,
the rail tracks were silver as knives in the frost.

All the stars hid their eyes as she yelped his name,
yes the stars hid their eyes as she yelped his name,
and old sickle moon sobbed behind clouds in shame.

She knelt in the dirt and she begged them to keep him,
a dog in the dirt she begged them to keep him,
Lord she howled in the dust and wept as they sent him.

Fifteen last week, he's lonesome and whip-thin,
no past, no home, he's lonesome and whip-thin,
sweet Jesus, the force of her tenderness cursed him.

Now they've sent him away on the dawn train to Wolfville,
her blackbird, her boy, on the dawn train to Wolfville,
and no wind can ever blow here but ill.

No, no wind can ever blow here but ill.

The Violets

Come to the dust, come, little one of us,
down with the fiddling crickets, come,

the sun streaming its light upon us,
shake and tremble, shudder in the rain drench,

salt-speckled, wind-blown,
our faces fresh as street-swept children.

Come o come and shake among us,
our scent so frighteningly sweet and dolorous,

down in the dust, come, o come to us,
a scent that haunts the heel that crushes it.

Home's not a place, you must believe this,
but one who names you and means beloved.

Prayer

In the long grass behind the chapel
the wind moans a blaming song.

Her heart, a dun bird in the chill evening light,
her breath making haloes;

all those she left behind crying in the night
like loons over the lake.

Come wings, carry her to the dark sleep,
to the moon with her mother's face,

that beautiful gone bone-orchard face.

The Book of Hours

He said he'd write to me

                        oh my love is a bird

when he found a new place.

                        a true-love bird

I'm waiting, Daniel

                        but they shot his poor heart

(are they hurting you?)

                        his poor bird heart

always waiting

                        and cut off his wings

as the leaves set the trees on fire.

A girl is a raindrop disappearing into the lake's beaten gold.

A girl is ivy in the arms of an indifferent tree, begging to be held.

A girl is a horseshoe nailed above the ruin's blown door.

A girl is the freckled egg hidden in the shit-crusted straw.

A girl is a swift, far gone, always sleeping on the wing.

A girl is a tinder box to light all the world's wanting.

Malagawatch

The beeches fell last night
in the high winds on the hill
over Malagawatch Cemetery.
We found them where they lay,
so slender, amongst the bracken,
their bodies the colour
of woodsmoke and pigeons.
We stood before them,
the mourning warblers chanting,
unable to believe that they had lived
for so long amongst us,
amongst our hemlock and maple,
been our shelter and dapple,
broomed our floors, raised our children,
yet had roots no deeper
than driftwood borne by the ocean.

. . .

I want to tell you about him now.
I want to tell about his hair
which was the colour of hay.
How it smelled like butter and grain.
How it was so silken between my fingers
that I have only touched such silk since
in a catkin or a child's hair.
I want to tell you about his skin,
which was freckled, for his mammy herself
was an orphan from Bonnybridge;
about his chest which was narrow
and blue from lack of goodness
and being beaten in the receiving home
for refusing to kneel.
I want to tell you about the down
on his forearms which turned gold in the sun
when we dug turnips at harvest.
I want to tell you about his teeth. His mouth.
I want to tell you that he did not pray
but tore the pages from his Bible
and threw them into the lake.
That he wrote each night to his sister in Glasgow
though he was barely book-learned
and the letters never posted.

That he kept a stolen knife in his trunk.
That if he'd stayed in Maryhill nothing good
could have come to him.
I want to tell you that he cried out in his sleep
for his mammy. That he bit his nails to the quick.
That he worked from cockcrow til blackout
and still they punished him, shut him out
in chill winds and ill weathers,
did not fetch the doctor for his fever
or give him linctus for his cough.
I want to tell you how they hated him
because they could not break him.
He spat in the milk the farmer's children drank
and his laugh was like a kite
I had seen once in Port Hood
which broke free from its strings.
I want to tell you that no one held me
with the care that he did, no one held me
as if I were a churn of cream to be worshipped
through eating, how when he looked at me
my body shed its fur and hooves
and was a girl's again.
I want to tell you everything now because
it is almost too late.
I want to tell you his name but oh –
his name, even now, dear Lord, I cannot say
his name without my heart feeling cracked –

And when I sit here in this chair
and think I have lived my whole life
to never have a home,
I send myself back to that hour in the woods
when he first took my fingers
and touched them to a leaf.
Feel it, he said. They call it a lamb's ear.
He was my wum then.
His name was Daniel McFadden.
And it was the softest thing I would ever feel.

Eliza in Cape Breton

Author's Note

This collection is loosely inspired by the story of my great-aunt Eliza Showell and her migration from the Middlemore Children's Emigration Homes in Birmingham to rural Cape Breton.

Some true facts about Eliza's journey lie in these pages but the narrative, as recounted here with its details of place, time, relationships and interior life, is an invention of my imagination. Any characters in these poems have no relation to an actual person, living or dead.

I am indebted to the many British Home Children and their families who have bravely shared their stories in letters, interviews and books. Their first-hand accounts have been integral to my imagining of Eliza's life.

For those who would like to know more about the British Home Children or who would like to trace the journeys of family members: https://www.britishhomechildren.com

Glossary

bibble / pebble
blart / cry
bone-orchard / cemetery
brew'us / wash house in back-to-back courts

canting / talking
clem-gutted / starving
cut / canal

donny / hand

fittle / food
fode / yard

glede / cinder
guttle / chew or gobble

jeth / death
jimmuck / shake

ketch / catch

leasowe/lezzer / meadow

midden / from privy midden, outdoor toilet
miskin / communal rubbish heap or dustbin

ommer / hammer
ond / hand
opple / apple
osses / horses
owd / old

pinna / pinafore dress

reisty / dirty or smelly

thrape / thrash
tranklements / little treasures, ornaments or bits and bobs

wammel / mongrel dog
wench / girl
wum / home

Bibliography

Bean, Philip & Melville, Joy. *Lost Children of the Empire: The Untold Story of Britain's Child Migrants* (Unwin Hyman, 1989)

Chinn, Carl. *Poverty Amidst Prosperity: The Urban Poor in England, 1834–1914* (Carnegie, 2007)

Hart, Valerie & Lyon, Rowena. *The Lost Children* (Balsall Heath Local History Society, 2020)

Haworth-Attard, Barbara. *Home Child* (Roussan, 1996)

Humphreys, Margaret. *Empty Cradles* (Corgi, 2011)

Kohli, Marjorie. *The Golden Bridge: Young Immigrants to Canada, 1833–1939* (Natural Heritage, 2003)

Little, Jean. *Orphan At My Door: The Home Child Diary of Victoria Cope* (Scholastic Canada, 2001)

Roberts-Pichette, Patricia. *Canadian Great Expectations: The Middlemore Experience* (Global Heritage Press, 2016)

Sources

The Middlemore Homes Archive, held by Birmingham Archives and Heritage at the Library of Birmingham

Canadian Museum of Immigration at Pier 21, Halifax

Acknowledgements

Poems in this book first appeared in *Ambit*, *Poetry*, *Poetry London* and *Poetry Review*.

Thanks to Clara Farmer, Parisa Ebrahimi, Amanda Waters and all at Chatto; to Gemma Trickey for her beautiful artwork; and to Chris Wellbelove.

Thank you to Val Hart and the Balsall Heath Local History Society for their guidance and their important work in bringing the stories of the Middlemore children to light. I'm grateful to Glyn Thomas for his detailed research into the story of the Showell family and to Dr Esther Asprey for her advice on dialect.

Deepest gratitude to the friends who offered their feedback on these poems: Fiona Benson, Jonathan Davidson, Hannah Lowe, Lucy Mercer, the Zellig Poets and always Declan Ryan.

With love and thanks to my family: especially Mom, who gifted me Eliza's story; my partner James, and Tom and Ted who fill our days with love.